Simon Says,
"Let's Play Learning Games"

written by Eunice M. Magos
and Esther H. Hornnes

illustrated by Priscilla Burris

EUNICE M. MAGOS received a Bachelor of Science degree from New York University, and a Master's degree in Individualized Education from the College of St. Scholastica in Minnesota. She has been a director of Head Start, taught gifted primary classes and participated in the Learning to Read Through the Arts program. She has taught remedial reading and kindergarten and currently teaches first grade in the Hopatcong Borough School District in New Jersey.

ESTHER H. HORNNES received a Bachelor of Arts degree from Shelton College and William Paterson College in New Jersey. She has done graduate work at North Dakota State University and Oslo University in Oslo, Norway. She has taught grades 1-4 and presently teaches pre-school in the Hillside Nursery School in Succasunna, New Jersey.

PRISCILLA BURRIS received an Associate of Arts degree in Creative Design from the Fashion Institute of Design and Merchandising in Los Angeles. As a free lance artist of child-related artwork, she has been drawing since she was one year old. Priscilla lives in southern California.

Copyright 1986 by THE MONKEY SISTERS, INC.
22971 Via Cruz
Laguna Niguel, CA 92677

ISBN 0-933606-41-9

INDOOR GAME PLAYER AWARD

had fun playing indoor games and learning the ABC's and 123's.

_____
Teacher

Simon Says, "Let's Play Learning Games"

This collection of games gives young children the experience of playing a group game while learning a basic readiness skill.

For each set of pages, there are game directions, suggested additional learning activities, and a work page to teach a specific skill. The games and related skills may be presented in any order to best meet your teaching needs.

These games which are suggested for indoor classroom activity may also be played in the school gymnasium and in some cases may also be suitable for outdoor activity.

Contents

Musical Chairs

Directions:

Arrange chairs with one less than the number of children playing. They should be in a side-by-side line with every other chair facing one direction and the others facing the opposite direction.

Children walk, march, or skip in the same direction around the chairs, as a piano or recorded music is played.

When the music stops, each child tries to sit in a chair. One child will be left without a chair. That child removes a chair from the end of the line and then sits on the side to watch the others.

The game continues until there is one chair left and two children playing. They walk around the chair to the music. The child who sits in the chair first, when the music stops, is the winner. If you prefer, you can stop with two winners and one chair remaining.

To add a festive theme at holiday times such as Halloween, Thanksgiving, Christmas, Valentine's Day, or Easter, you can play songs to suit the occasion. Each child may wear a headband decorated with seasonal art as they play. Those who are eliminated from the game and are now sitting on the side may want to clap and sing to the music.

Name _____

Sound-O

Directions: Teacher prepares one set of cards for use by caller. For class use, each child gets a copy and cuts out 9 large squares and rearranges them in random order so each child's SOUND-O card will be different. These are pasted onto a blank paper. The 12 small cards are cut apart. Caller (or teacher) makes the sound indicated by the object on the card. Players use their cards to match and cover the correct pictures on the SOUND-O board. The first child to cover 3 in a row—horizontally, vertically, or diagonally—is the winner. That child must call out SOUND-O! For variety, children may be asked to cover corners only, the entire card, the middle row horizontally, etc. (There are small cards that have extra sounds not shown on large squares.)

Hot Potato

Directions:

The children sit in a circle. When the music begins, they pass the potato around the circle as quickly as they can. When the music stops, the one holding the potato is out of the game. He must go and sit in the middle of the circle. When the music begins again, they start passing the potato once more. When the music stops, the same thing happens—the one holding the potato must join the other person in the middle of the circle. This continues until you have only one person left. That child is the winner.

You could also play this game during a holiday time substituting the potato with things such as: a small pumpkin, a candy cane, a plastic Easter egg, etc.

You might also like to do a science activity learning about the potato—when you plant them, where you plant them, how they grow, etc.

Simon Says, "Let's Play Learning Games" © THE MONKEY SISTERS, INC.

Name _____

Mr. Potato

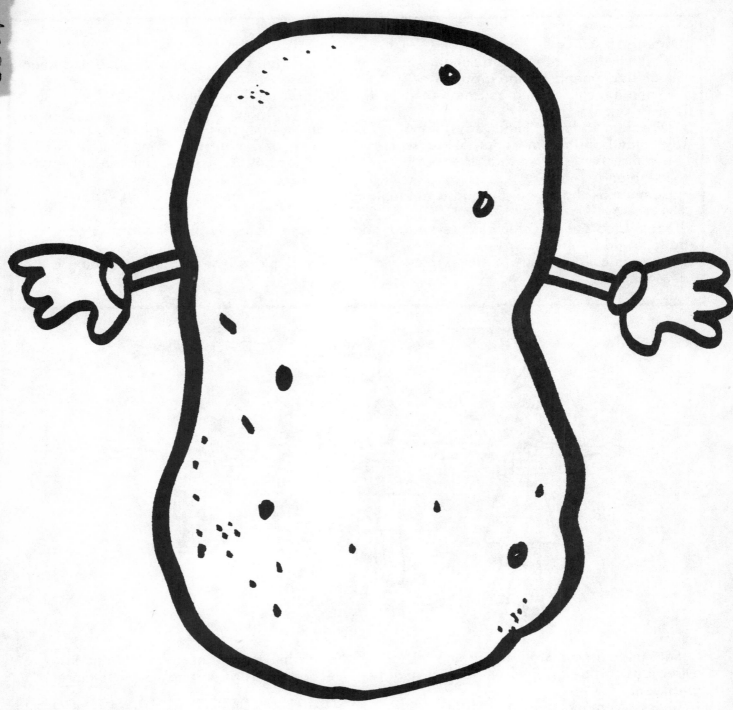

Draw two BLUE eyes on Mr. Potato.
Draw a BLACK nose on Mr. Potato.
Draw a RED mouth on Mr. Potato.
Color Mr. Potato BROWN.

Simon Says

Directions:

One child is chosen to be Simon. The other children stand so that they can see and hear Simon's commands to the group.

When the child acting as Simon gives a direction preceded by "Simon Says," the group is to follow along.

Directions include "Simon says, hands on hips; Simon says, stand on one foot; Simon says, stand on the other foot, Simon says, run in place, or Simon says, arms straight out."

If a direction is given that does not begin with "Simon says," then the children are not to follow along.

Commands should be given in a random manner using "Simon says" or NOT using "Simon says."

Simon acts out all commands, even though only those preceded by "Simon says" are to be followed by the group.

When a child makes a mistake, that child sits down in place. The last child standing is the new Simon.

For children who are just learning this game, the teacher may want to be the leader. Directions can be given slowly at first and then speeded up as the group becomes more proficient.

Quick commands such as "Stop!", "Sit!", or "Hop!" are a challenge and add to the fun.

Also, this game can be as inactive or active as you choose from "wiggle your nose" or "blink your eyes" to "jump up and down" or "clap your hands."

As a variation to promote listening skills Simon can give commands, but not act out any of the actions.

Making a SIMON SAYS chart will motivate inventiveness and keep the game interesting. Each time a child directs the group with a new action, that action is recorded on the chart. The chart then becomes a resource for motion ideas throughout the year.

Name _____

Simon Bear

Follow these directions and color Simon Bear.

Simon says: "Color the bow tie GREEN."

Simon says: "Color the hat BLUE."

Simon says: "Color the heart RED."

Simon says: "Color the balloon YELLOW."

Simon says: "Color the ears ORANGE."

Simon says: "Color me BROWN."

Call Ball

This is a good get-acquainted game to play in the beginning of the year. You can vary the way of throwing the ball. You might want the children to sit down and have the child in the middle roll the ball to the person whose name he calls.

Name _____

Find the Matching Pairs

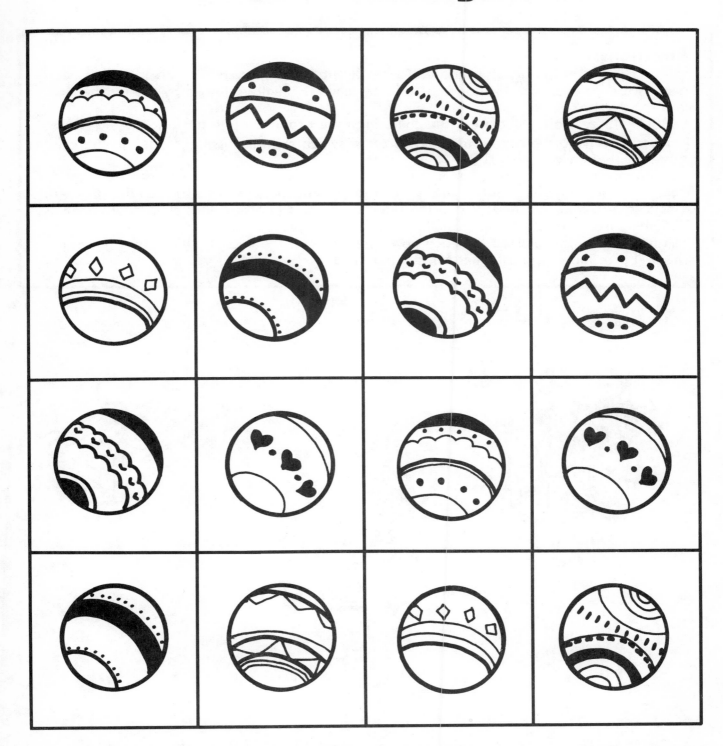

Directions: Children cut squares out and turn them over with blank side up. Child picks any two squares and turns them over. If they match, child gets to keep them. If they do not match, turn them down and try again. Children should be urged to try and remember where the matching balls are once they are turned over. Game continues until each child has matched all the pairs.

Who's Missing?

You can change this into a memory game involving objects by having the children place a selection of items such as crayons, scissors, pencils, and blocks in front of each of them. IT studies the items and leaves the room. The leader tells which object is to be removed and held behind the children's backs. IT returns and tries to guess the missing item.

Simon Says, "Let's Play Learning Games" © THE MONKEY SISTERS, INC.

Name _____

What's Missing?

Directions: See if children can remember objects in their environment. Children cut out pictures below and paste them into the correct scene.

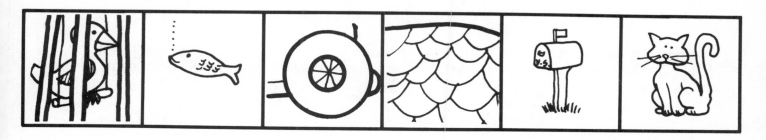

Fox and Squirrels

Directions:
Number the children off in groups of three. Have two of them hold hands to form the tree. The third child will be a squirrel who will live in that tree. Make sure that groups of children are spread out so they are not close to each other. One child is chosen to be a fox and another child to be a squirrel without a home. The fox chases the squirrel who runs to a tree to get in. When this happens, the squirrel in the tree must leave immediately and the fox chases this squirrel. If the fox catches a squirrel before he gets in a tree, he becomes the fox and the original fox becomes a squirrel.

You might want to compare the fox with a squirrel as to: where they live, what they eat, their size, their appearance. It would be interesting to put this information on a chart as the children contribute information.

Find the Twins!

Directions: Children use same color crayon to color the two in each row that are alike. As they color an animal, you might want to discuss that animal with them. If you have pictures of places these animals live in, you can let the children match a home with an animal.

Alphabet Race

Directions:

Divide the group into two or three teams depending on the number of children playing. Choose a portion of the alphabet that the children are familiar with. You can divide the alphabet into three sections: A to H, I to Q, and R to Z. Play using letters from one section at a time.

Place a set of capital letters for each team in slightly hidden but obvious places around the room. The letters can be hidden before the children arrive or while they are hiding their eyes. Put another set of letters along the chalk ledge so that the children will know which letters they are looking for.

On a signal, the first member of each team searches for the first letter in sequence. When it is found, the next child searches. The first team to find all the hidden letters in their set is the winner.

You can adapt this game to finding cards or objects with beginning sounds, colors, shapes, or numbers. Be sure to put a sample set of cards on the ledge and if you are using real objects in the room, check to see that there are enough items that will match.

For example: if the children were searching for colors, and you had three teams, then you would want to have at least three red objects within reach of the children.

Alphabet Race Track Game

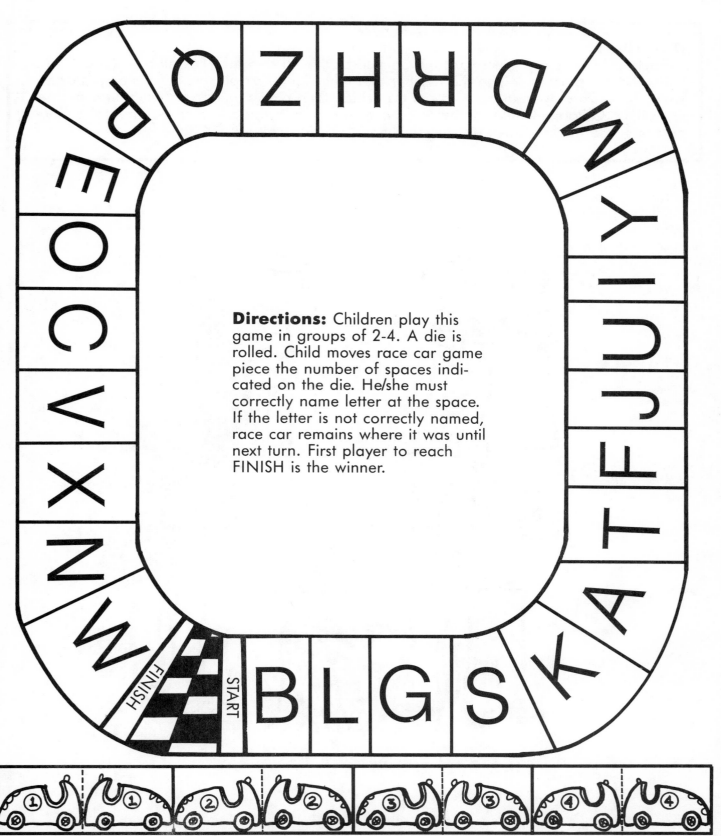

Directions: Children play this game in groups of 2-4. A die is rolled. Child moves race car game piece the number of spaces indicated on the die. He/she must correctly name letter at the space. If the letter is not correctly named, race car remains where it was until next turn. First player to reach FINISH is the winner.

Game pieces: Cut on solid lines. Fold on dotted lines. Each player is given an assigned number car, or cars may each be made a different color.

Back-to-Back

Back-to-Back Match!

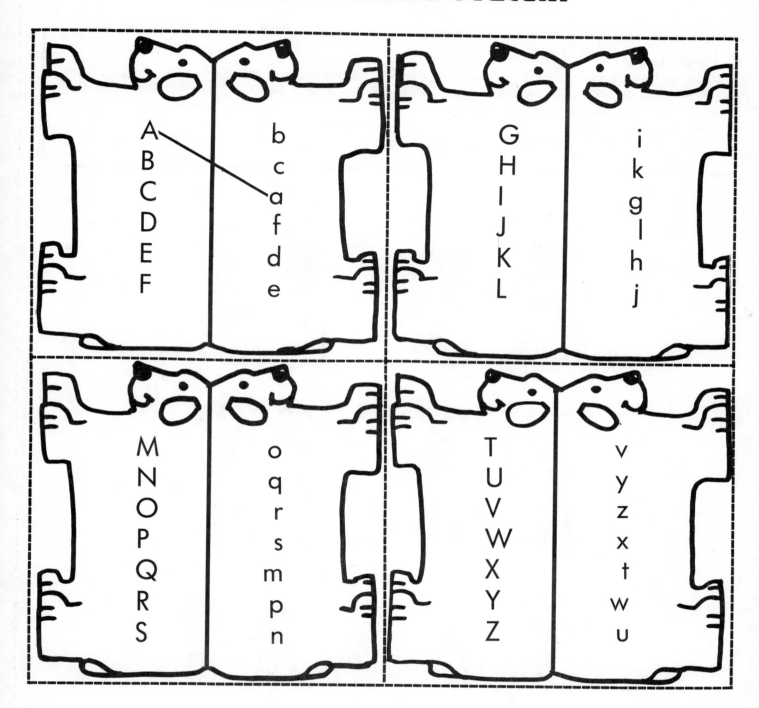

A B C D E F   b c a f d e

G H I J K L   i k g l h j

M N O P Q R S   o q r s m p n

T U V W X Y Z   v y z x t w u

Directions: Children match the upper and lower case letters by drawing a line between them. Then children may color the dogs. Cut apart on the dotted lines, then fold each one on the solid line so they will stand up.

Beanbag Indoor Relay

Directions:
  Form three lines of children. Give a beanbag to the child at the beginning of each line.
  On a signal, the beanbag is passed down the line from beginning to end. When the last child has the beanbag, that child runs to the front of the line and quickly passes the beanbag back. Each child in turn repeats this sequence.
  The winning team is the one where the first child is back at the original lead position.

  You can vary the game by having beanbags passed in different ways: over the head, through the legs, to the right side, to the left side, etc.

Name _____

Alphabet Express

c

fg

j

mn

qr

uv

CABOOSE

Directions: Children cut out alphabet squares. They paste them on the correct cars in sequence. Then they cut out the train on the solid lines. Paste the sections together. Fan fold on dotted lines so that the train can stand!

| hi | wx | ab | op | yz | de | st | kl |

Stoop Tag

Directions:
   The players are spread out in the playing area. One child is IT. He/she tries to tag another player. When the player who is being chased stoops down, he is 'safe' and IT can't tag him. When a player is tagged, he must call out, "I'm IT" and the game continues. You might like to try having two or three children be IT at the same time.

Simon Says, "Let's Play Learning Games" © THE MONKEY SISTERS, INC.

Which Ones Match?

Directions: Children look at the illustration on the left. Ask what sound the object begins with. Children color the pictures on the right that begin with the same sound. They may cross out the ones that do not begin with the same sound.

Mouse Trap

Directions:

A circle is formed with half of the group holding hands. This is the 'mouse trap.' When joined hands are raised, the trap is open. When joined hands are lowered, the trap is closed.

A leader is chosen from the children in the second half of the group and the remaining children are the 'mice.'

Begin the game with the trap open. Mice weave in and out of the trap. The leader says, "Snap!" Hands are lowered, and the trap closes.

Those mice trapped inside the circle become part of the trap. A child who tries to break through the trap also becomes part of the trap.

The game continues as the leader says, "Trap open!" or "Snap!" at the appropriate time.

Players who were mice originally become the trap, and players who were the trap become the mice once all the mice are caught.

A new leader is selected each time all of the mice are caught.

You could play "Birds in the Cage" with "Cage open!" or "Cage closed!" Children who are birds must imitate flying as they go in and out of the cage.

Name _____

Mouse and Friend

Climb the ladder to the cheese!

Go down the ladder to win!

Go in and out of the holes!

Directions: Children play in pairs. Letter squares below are cut apart and arranged in a random pile, face down. Players take turns drawing from the pile. Using a small chip or marker, player moves to next picture that has the same beginning sound as shown on the square turned over. Child names item and says the beginning letter. (fan, moon, milk, five, monkey, fish, four, mitten, map, football, mop, fox)

m	m	m	m	m	m
f	f	f	f	f	f

Squirrel and Nut

Directions:

The children can either sit in circle formation or stand in circle formation with their hands open behind their backs. One child will be the squirrel and will go around the circle and drop a nut (can be a crayon or a piece of chalk, etc.) into someone's hand. This child must immediately run after the squirrel and try to tag him before he gets to the vacated spot of the second child. If the squirrel does not get caught, the second child becomes the squirrel.

To help review the consonant sounds while playing this game, you might ask the child to give a word beginning with 'N' or 'V' when the nut is dropped in their hand and before they can run after the squirrel. If this is done, the squirrel must wait until the word is given before he/she starts running around the circle.

Squirrel Hunt

Directions: Children hunt for hidden pictures. They color all pictures beginning with 'N' red and all pictures beginning with 'V' blue. (Items to find are: newspaper, nest, nut, nine, nail, vase, vest, van, violin, valentine.)

Huckle, Buckle Beanstalk

Directions:

An object is selected to be hidden. A child is chosen to be IT. All of the children except IT leave the area or close their eyes so that they cannot see where the object will be hidden.

IT hides the object in plain sight. Then the other children return, or open their eyes, and begin to search. As each child spots the hidden object, the child should not look directly at it or tell the others where it is. Instead, the child goes to a seat and says, "Huckle, Buckle, Beanstalk." Each child who finds the object continues on with the game in the same manner.

After all the children have found the object, the first child that spotted it goes to the object and then becomes IT to hide it the next time.

When the children are searching, it may become apparent that some children are having difficulty finding the object. Clues can be given that will reinforce rhyming concepts. "It is near something that begins with 'c' and rhymes with boat." (near the coat) "It is near something that begins with 'f' and rhymes with dish." (near the fish)

Name _____

Time to Rhyme

Directions: Children cut out the squares above and paste the pictures on the animal names that rhyme with it. As an extra, animals may be stapled to a folded paper plate to make roly-poly rocking animals.

Doggy, Doggy, Where's Your Bone?

Directions:

One child is selected to be the dog. He/she sits on a stool or chair in front of the other children but with his/her back facing them. The dog's bone is an eraser or book which is placed on the floor near the chair.

The teacher tells one of the children, by either a nod of the head or by tapping on the shoulder, that they should sneak up and try to steal the bone from the dog. If the dog hears someone coming, he/she must say ''Bow-wow.'' The child that is stealing the bone must return to his seat. The teacher selects others to try to steal the bone. If a child succeeds in getting the bone before the dog barks, all the children say, ''Doggy, doggy, where's your bone? Somebody stole it from your home!''

The dog must try to guess who took his bone and this child will get to be the next dog.

Bone

Dog

This would be a good time to talk about pets and how you should take care of them. Ask what dogs eat and how often you should feed them.

Name _____

What Do We Like to Eat?

Directions: Children cut out the pictures below and match them with the correct animal by pasting them in the square. Children may color page.

Have You Seen My Sheep?

Directions:
   Have children sit in a circle facing toward the center. One child is chosen to be the shepherd and walk around the outside of the circle behind the children. The shepherd stops behind one of the children and asks, "Have you seen my sheep?"

   That child replies,"What does your sheep look like?"

   The shepherd then describes another child sitting in the circle. When the child guesses who is being described, both get up. The child that guessed becomes IT. IT chases the child that was described with both children running in a clockwise direction.

   IT tries to tag the other child before he/she can get back to the space that was vacated. In the meantime, the shepherd sits in ITS space to be out of the way of the chase.

   IT becomes the new shepherd if the other child is tagged. If the other child gets back to the vacated space before being tagged, then that child is the new shepherd.

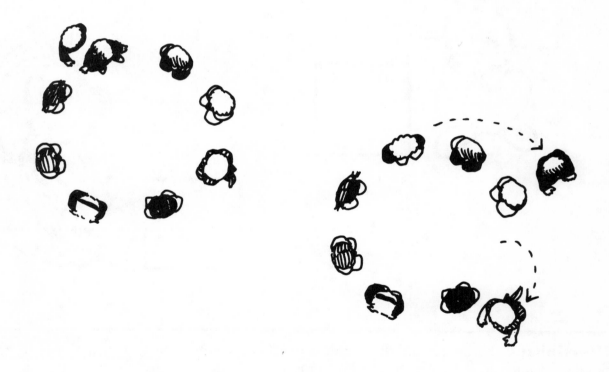

   You may want to review various aspects that make one child different in appearance from another. Clues that could be used would be boy or girl, hair color, eye color, dress, glasses, etc.

   If the teacher begins the game as the first shepherd, the children can more readily understand how to give the clues.

   Everyone has to listen carefully to the clues so that the child who is being described will know who he/she is and be ready to run as soon as he/she is guessed.

Guess Which One!

1. It is furry and says, "Meow."

A.   B.   C.

2. He is big and likes to smile.

A.   B.   C.

3. It has feathers and likes the water.

A.   B.   C.

4. It is cold and looks like a person.

A.   B.   C.

5. She has curly hair and likes to skate.

A.   B.   C.

6. It has a long tail and eats nuts.

A.   B.   C.

Directions: Children color the picture in each row that is described as the clues are read aloud.

Answers: 1.B   2.C   3.A   4.C   5.A   6.B

Hide the Beanbag

Simon Says, "Let's Play Learning Games" © THE MONKEY SISTERS, INC.

Name _____

Find the Shapes!

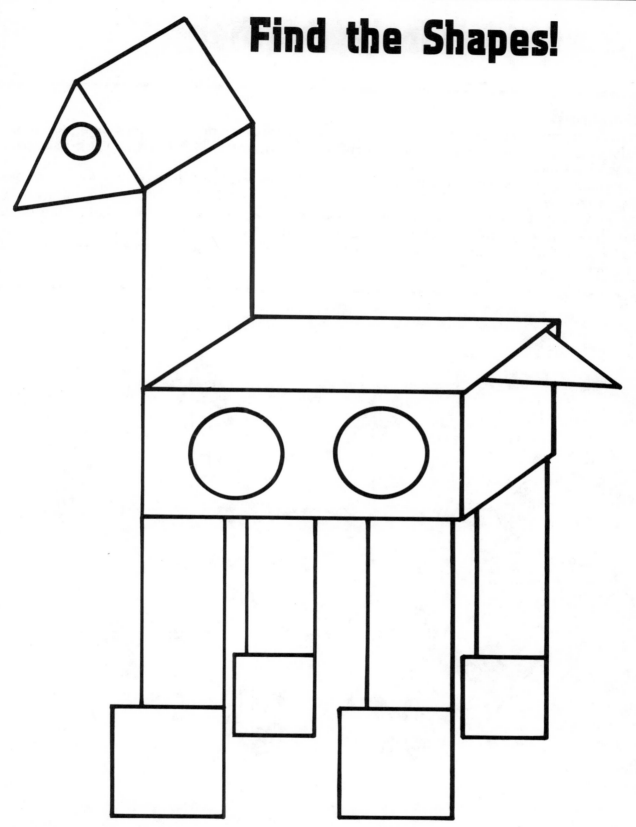

Directions: Children color the triangles red, the squares blue, the circles yellow, and the rectangles green.

Circle Football

Directions:

Children sit in a circle so that they are facing the center and have legs extended in a V-shape. One child begins by rolling a rubber ball across the circle so that it passes over a large circle marked in the center.

A child across the circle then tries to 'catch' the ball with his/her feet by closing his/her legs when the ball comes directly toward him.

A catch with the legs does not count. One point is given for any catch below the ankles. The child who receives the ball then rolls it to another child across the circle. In order for the child rolling the ball to know who still has not had a turn, players who have not had a turn may raise their hand to signal.

Children who do not get the ball over the circle shape as it crosses the circle could be required to give up a point. This would then be a good game to reinforce plus and minus concepts.

Name _____

Favorite Sports

Soccer

Baseball

Tennis

Sailing

Football

Ice Skating

Directions: Children cut out shapes in squares and match them in the appropriate sport.

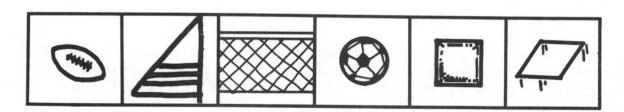

It's Your Choice!

Directions:
    One child is chosen to be IT. All the other children stand on a line facing IT. Have four or five different size balls laying on the floor by the child who is IT. IT can choose the size ball he/she wants to throw to each child. He says the name of the child and throws the ball to the first child on his left. The child then throws the ball back to IT. IT then proceeds to throw the ball to the next child and so on down the line until all have had a chance to catch and throw the ball. The children try to make good throws and catches. When the line is finished, the first child on the left gets to be the next IT. For succeeding rounds, the next child in line is IT.

    For variety, you may try using different size beanbags instead of balls. This will eliminate running after a ball a child has missed. You could also have IT say what size ball or beanbag he is using: "I'm going to use the smallest ball" or "I'm going to use the largest beanbag" etc.

Simon Says, "Let's Play Learning Games" © THE MONKEY SISTERS, INC.

Name _____

Big or Little?

1.

2.

3.

4.

5.

6.

Directions: Read these directions aloud as children complete each task:
1. Look at box 1. Color the hat on the smallest clown red.
2. Look at box 2. Color the largest tent brown.
3. Look at box 3. Color the medium size present green.
4. Look at box 4. Circle the smallest kite. Color it blue.
5. Look at box 5. Color the largest flower yellow.
6. Look at box 6. Put a red X on the medium size house.

Hit the Bucket

Directions:

Children stand in a circle facing the middle. Place a waste basket or bucket in the center. One player is chosen to stand in the circle by the bucket.

A ball is given to a player on the circle. That player tries to throw the ball into the bucket. A point is awarded if the player is successful. The player in the middle retrieves the ball and passes it to the next player in the circle.

Player or players with the highest score after the same number of turns are the winners. Each child can keep his own score or a scorekeeper can be chosen.

Vary the size of the circle so that the distance from players to the basket continues to be challenging to your group. As the children increase their skill, you may want to enlarge the circle.

The size of the balls that are used can be varied. If three different-sized balls are used, the large ball can be worth 1 point, the middle size ball 2 points, and the smallest ball 3 points. Children choose the size ball they want to use and determine the highest possible number of points that they can win.

Name _____

Big or Small, Match Them All!

Directions: Children draw lines to match the small and large objects that go together.

Four Corners

Name _____

1 - 2 - 3 - 4

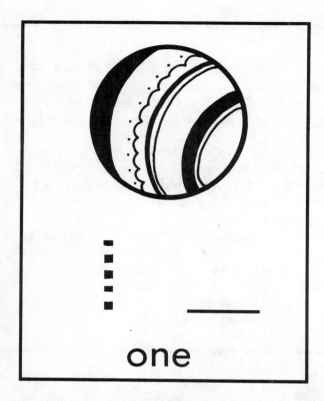

one

two

three

four

Directions: Children count the objects in each box. They trace the number on the dotted line and write the number on the line. They may color the objects and cut out four boxes to make into a mini-booklet.

Seven Up

Directions:

Children sit scattered about the room. They may use the floor, a chair, or sit at a desk. Seven of the children are chosen to stand facing the group. The remaining children put their heads in their hands and cover their eyes so that they can't see the seven as they walk about the room. Those children who are covering their eyes put the thumb of one hand pointing up in view of those children who are IT.

The seven children who are IT do not hide their eyes, but walk around until they select a child who is sitting. The IT child carefully folds down the thumb of a sitting child and tries not to give away any clues about his/her identity. When all seven children have selected a different child and are again standing and facing the group, the teacher says, "Heads up. Children who had their thumbs folded down may stand up."

Then each child in turn tries to guess who it was that touched their thumb. The group of seven is carefully looked at for any indications. If the guess is correct, then the two children change places. Continue until all who are standing have had their chance to guess.

Those children who were not correctly guessed then disclose the name of the child that they had picked. These players and the new players now continue for another round. To be IT, a child must correctly identify who it was that pushed down his/her thumb.

If the group is very small, you can adapt this game by having only four up, etc.

This can be an on-going game by listing on the chalkboard the current players who are 'up.' Number a list from 1-7. Record the players that were 'up' when the game ended. Change the list at the end of each day's game. Children like to play this game as a "to be continued" game.

41.   Simon Says, "Let's Play Learning Games" © THE MONKEY SISTERS, INC.

Name _____

Farmyard Friends

1 ------ Paste	**2** ------ Paste	**3** ------ Paste
4 ------ Paste	**5** ------ Paste	**6** ------ Paste

7 ------ Paste	

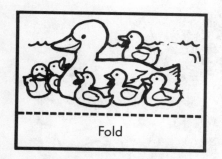
Fold

Fold

Fold

Fold

Fold

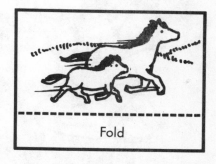
Fold

Directions: Children count the farm animals in each box. Then they paste the farmyard animal on the correct number. Fold and paste to make stand-ups.

Fold

Simon Says, "Let's Play Learning Games" © THE MONKEY SISTERS, INC.

Wonder Ball

The wonder ball goes round and round,
To pass it quickly you are bound.
If you're the one to hold it last,
You are O-U-T, out!

Directions:

The children sit in a circle and say the poem as the ball is passed around from one child to another. The one holding the ball when the last word of the poem is said, is out of the game. Continue to play until all the children but one are out.

Name _____

Make A Wonder Wheel

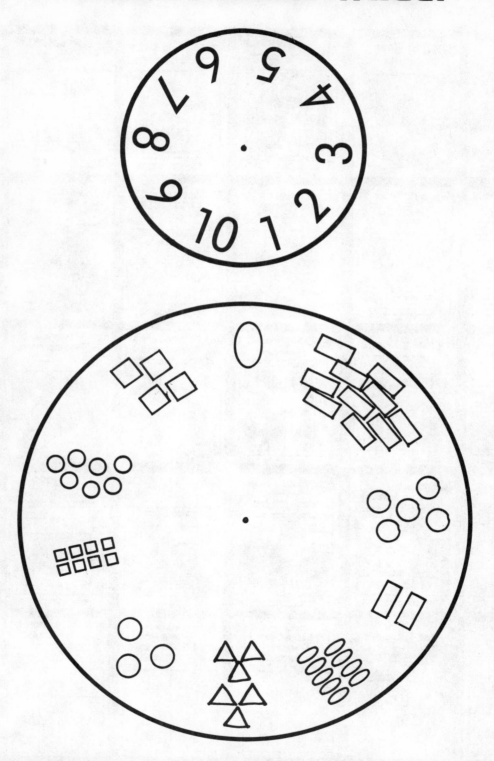

Directions: Children cut out the circles and put them together with a brad. Then they move the circles to match the number with the correct set of objects. Children may color each set a different color.

See your local school supply dealer for these products by THE MONKEY SISTERS